JOURNAL

ONE A DAY
QUOTES
TO
DESTINY

DETERMINATION FUELS THE SUCCESS
OF A DESIRED DREAM!

JOURNAL

ONE A DAY QUOTES TO DESTINY

Published by:

Inspirational Hopes

P.O Box 4002 (G.P.O)

Castries, LC04 101

Saint Lucia, West Indies

Mailing and inquiries from local, regional, UK, and Europe can be sent to the above address.

Mailing and inquiries from USA, Canada, and other locations send to:

Inspirational Hopes

7701 NW 15th Street

Suite# LC916000

Miami, Florida 33106

ISBN 978-976-96533-2-0

www.Inspirationalhopes.com

Printed in the United States of America

Cover Design: Vanessa Mendozzi

Interior Design: Natalia Junqueira (Dawn Book Design)

Journaling to Destiny

This Journal belongs to:

____

Don't wonder about your future. Create one!

Sometimes we spend so much time worrying
about tomorrow when we could be planning
for it and working hard toward it.
Put pen on paper, write the vision,
and execute it!

Persistence and pursuit is the process
of birthing our dreams.

*Don't let the day define itself to you, but
you define your day!*

*What you are learning now is the
foundation for your future.
Learn all you can now!*

Hop back aboard the train of dreams,
and begin to dream and hope again.

Don't allow your weaknesses to
overcome your destiny.

Set out a plan and strategy to bring forth dreams and visions.

With a plan before you, you focus on the main thing; it serves as a reminder of where you desire to be in the future and leads you to positive action in getting there.
So plan it, write it, and work at it!

The most miserable person in life is
one without a purpose and a passion.

Greatness is within you;
don't give up on you!

*Your past is nothing compared to your
future, for your future is greater
than your past.*

*Don't waste time around people who
bring out the worst in you,
but invest time in those who bring out
the best in you.*

To get something accomplished,
discipline must be present.

If you are able to
conquer the
little things,
then the big things
become nothing to
overcome.

Be consistent, and go hard!

Don't allow laziness to creep into your life. It is a big dream killer and the seed of poverty.

Sleep is your body's best friend, but
excess sleep is an enemy to your
success!

Resilience: it's a force to reckon with.

Faith is hoping for what is not yet
manifested but knowing that God will
keep His promise.

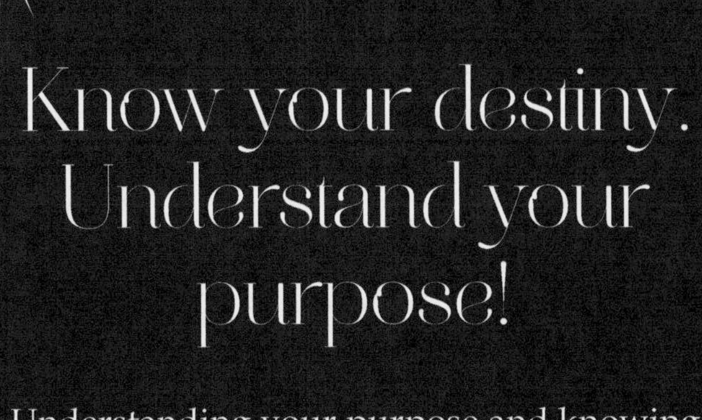

Know your destiny. Understand your purpose!

Understanding your purpose and knowing your destiny in life keeps you grounded.

*Don't allow people to take control of
your sail; they will lead you down
oceans and streams where you never
intended to go.*

You may not have much in your hands,
but within you is greatness.

Starting is one thing, but finishing is everything.

Don't look at the size of your mountain.
Just start climbing; eventually you will
make it to the top.

One A Day Quotes To Destiny

One a Day Quotes to Destiny (Series One) is concentrated with thoughts of wisdom for everyday living. These quotes can help you stay motivated and focused on achieving your goals and dreams. Just as a life coach guides and instructs their clients so they can live to their full potential, so does One a Day Quotes to Destiny.

Everyone on earth has a specific purpose and destination in life, and one who lives life outside of their purpose can go through life feeling miserable and unsatisfied. These quotes will help build strength, resilience, and determination in the specific areas of business, life's purpose, dreams, and mentorship, so that every day can be lived on purpose and with a purpose in mind.

ISBN 978-976-96533-0-6 (Paperback)

ISBN 978-976-96533-1-3 (Ebook)

Learn more about author and connect on social media
www.teespring.com/stores/inspirational-hopes

- Facebook: Inspirational Hopes

- Instagram: Inspirational.Hopes

- Website: www.Janakalexander.com